freebie.robloxiakid.com/r

My dearest fans
and reviewers:

ROBLOXIA KID

YTAHA
Coolalto940
Diamondminer168
Dragonfire
Tobi Salami
Ellen Henry
Natalija F.
JU

THANK YOU!!!

Unofficial

Diary of a Roblox Noob: Christmas Special

Robloxia Kid

Contents

Entry #1:

Ho, Ho, Ho! Merry Pizza!

"Order up!"

The sound of a bell rang through the air and a group of hungry customers turned their heads towards the counter. All of them were eager to get their hot and steamy pizzas, straight out of the oven. Yep, it was a really, really busy day at the pizza place in the Work at a Pizza Place server. In fact, this was probably the busiest day we've ever seen... ever!

I was still pretty new to the Work at a Pizza Place server, although I was loving every minute of it.

Hey, they don't call me "Noob" for nothing! I'm always exploring new servers, trying out new games and checking out new and exciting stuff.

You guys are probably already aware of my adventures at this point...

I've had a lot of action packed adventures now, haven't I?

I wanted to take a small break from all of the action and kind of kick back and relax a bit.

And what better place to do just that than the Work at a Pizza Place server?

This place was just absolutely awesome!

I got to cook up some pretty great tasting pizzas for the customers while getting some of that pizza for myself...

I got to ride around the whole neighborhood,

delivering pizzas from door to door while seeing all of the cool sights...

I also got to save up my money and get a pretty cool crib not to far from the pizza place!

And Work at a Pizza Place isn't just all about working and serving the customers, you know!

I also get to go out on weekends and spend the whole night chilling out and dancing to some awesome tunes at the coolest place in the server: Party Island!

Yep, things were going pretty well for me...

Well, that was until, those weird robbers showed up.

But I digress... I haven't even told you guys the whole story yet! Let's go back to the present now, shall we?

"Is that my pizza?" one of the hungry customers eagerly asked the cashier who stood at the counter.

"Yes sir, that's definitely yours! One Tomato Craze Pizza with extra cheese! Enjoy!" the cashier said happily.

The customer quickly swiped his pizza away from the cashier like a man who had just spotted a piece of gold. There were several other customers behind him who watched in jealousy as he walked away to enjoy his delicious pizza.

Today was a lot busier compared to the others, probably because Christmas was just around the corner!

Yep, you heard me right! It was almost Christmas! And the Christmas season always seemed to bring in the hungriest customers from every corner of the whole server.

I would usually get busy on a normal day inside the kitchen, pumping out some awesome tasting pizzas for the hungry customers. But since Christmas was getting pretty close, today was different. I wasn't just going to bake pizzas... I was going to decorate the entire restaurant with some awesome Christmas decorations!

"Noob! Get over here kid!" the store manager said.

Our store manager, Santy was a large and portly dude with a really thick, white beard to match. Now that I think about it, he actually kind of looked like Santa Claus.

"Yes sir!" I said as I quickly made my way over to Santy the manager.

"Take these wreaths and hang them on every corner you can find! Make sure to come back to me once you're done." he said happily.

Santy handed me some large, green, leafy wreaths that had some colorful ribbons tied to them. The wreaths definitely looked like a great addition to the restaurant in order to spread the Christmas spirit around.

"Aye aye, sir!" I said.

Santy smiled at me and nodded his head.

All of my co-workers always said that Santy had loved the Christmas season. It was his favorite time of the year, and it showed!They said that he was always a lot nicer whenever Christmas was just around the corner, and I could tell that he was being extra nice to me too!

"Hey Noob! You gonna hang those wreaths up?" one of my co-workers in the restaurant said.

"Yeah... I figured these will help to spread the Christmas spirit around!" I said happily.

My co-worker smiled and nodded his head.

"Yeah... Christmas is just around the corner now, ain't it? It's gonna be awesome! Just think of the presents we're all gonna get!"

"Christmas isn't all about presents, dude! It's about just being chill and happy because it's everyone's got the Christmas spirit!"

My co-worker let out a friendly laugh and smiled.

I went on with my task and hung the wreaths around as many doors and windows inside the restaurant that I could find. When I went back to Santy the manager for my next task, he gave me a couple of christmas lights that were attached to some really, really long wires. He told me to hang them up in close to the ceiling and to turn them on to spread even more of the Christmas joy!

Yep, you could really feel the Christmas

season inside the pizza parlor. But the pizza restaurant wasn't the only place that had the Christmas spirit all around it...

Just about the entire server of the Work at a Pizza Place had a Christmas feel to it! The entire city was covered with some cool and soft snow, and almost every house in the entire neighborhood had a colorful and unique wreath hanging on the top of their doors.

Everyone was happy, and you could see that people were getting eager to greet the year's annual Christmas event.

Christmas is just awesome, plain and simple! Don't you think?

I'm sure you guys love Christmas as much as I do too...

But apparently, there are some people in the server who don't like Christmas at all!

Now who in the world wouldn't like Christmas?!

Read on and you guys will find out soon enough...

Entry # 2:

Now Where Did All These Guys Come From?!

It was another totally busy day at the pizza parlor with tons and tons of customers coming in and out, ordering the craziest flavors we had to offer. We were another day closer to Christmas and it just seemed to get busier and busier the closer we got to the big event!

Even though we had a lot more customers than usual, me and my co-workers were more than happy to serve them all with their favorite pizzas and food.

However, we didn't expect what would actually happen next.

Our portly and cheery store manager, Santy, suddenly walked towards the counter and had a big smile on his face. He was obviously going to announce something big. Was it going to be the date of the big annual Christmas party? Or were we going to get a raise because Christmas was getting closer and closer? I honestly wanted the raise... Hey, I still needed to pay for that awesome new house that I had just bought within the city, you know!

"All right guys. I want everyone's attention!" Santy said aloud.

All of the pizza parlor's employees turned their attention towards the large man who really looked like Santa Claus. I mean, he really did look like him. I bet you that he probably did that on purpose or something...

"What's the big fuss all about?" Jonesy said.

Jonesy was the first guy I had made friends with when I started working here at the Work at a Pizza Place server. He was a pretty cool dude, and we've been best friends ever since. He loves to party at party island, just like me, and we both share a love for really fast cars! I even promised to take him back to Robloxia some day so he can check out my totally awesome hotrod car.

"I'm not really sure... let's see what ol' Santy's got to say this time!" I said.

"As all of you probably already know, we've been getting a lot of customers lately. And everyone knows that's because Christmas is just around the corner! And boy... this couldn't have come at a better time!" he said.

"Are you going to give us a bigger salary?" one of our co-workers said eagerly.

Santy shook his head and sighed.

"No... not just yet. But I've got something better for you guys..."

"The Christmas Party?! When's it going to happen?" another one of our co-workers asked.

"Settle down, settle down! No, it's not going to be a raise... nor is it going to be the announcement of the Christmas party this year. Today, you guys are going to get five new co-workers!" Santy said happily.

Five new co-workers?! Whoah! Now where in the world did they come from?!

Everyone in the counter seemed just as surprised as I did! The most number of new workers we'd ever gotten in a single day was two! And we didn't get any new employees for a long time after that!

"Dude! Did you hear that?! Five new co-workers in one day! That's crazy!" Jonesy told me.

I shook my head in disbelief. I couldn't believe it either! Where did all those new employees come from? I didn't really mind having a couple of new helping hands around with the customers... but five of them?! Something just wasn't right here.

"I know, dude! Something's going on here... And I'm going to find out just what it is!" I said.

Just before anyone else could say anything more, five really big and mean looking dudes suddenly walked through the back door of the restaurant. They didn't exactly look like nice people, if you know what I mean...

All five of them had really large muscles, and all of them had tattoos on their necks. They also had really rough and rugged looking beards on their faces. They actually looked more suited to be bodyguards than a bunch of people working at a quaint little pizza store.

"Oh, here are the newest employees of the Work at a Pizza Place! Just in time for the introductions!" Santy said eagerly as he presented the ten scary looking guys who just entered the restaurant.

"Everyone, welcome our newest team members to the pizza restaurant crew! This is Rojack, Cobra, Conard, Lombard and Jackson! I can't actually remember your full names, though. Actually, your resumes didn't even have your full names listed when I inspected them... but who cares? Welcome to the team, guys! All five of you have already went through training, so have fun with the job and good luck!" Santy said before making his way out of the counter and kitchen area and going inside the manager's room.

Lucky for him, he didn't have to deal with these really scary looking dudes!

"Uhh... is it just me, Jonesy... or do these guys look more like criminals than pizza employees?" I whispered over to Jonesy.

"Aw, come on dude! I mean, I know they look real rough around the edges... but we can't judge them because of the way they look! They're probably really nice guys once you get to know them." Jonesy said.

I wasn't too sure if I wanted to agree with Jonesy. I honestly thought that he was being a little bit too positive. And besides, something just didn't add up! How did get five new employees into the restaurant all of a sudden? And why did all of them look like they just robbed a bank or something? And why didn't they even put in their full names on their resume?!

There was definitely something fishy about

all of this...

And I was going to get to the bottom of it, one way or another!

Christmas was already just around the corner, and I wasn't about to let something like this ruin the best Christmas ever!

There was only one way to find out more about this whole thing...

Make friends!

And that's where I'm really, really good at.

But just before anyone even had a chance to talk, the sound of a bell ringing through the air suddenly entered everyone's ears. There was yet another order from another hungry customer, and all of us had to resume working.

"All right, everyone! Let's get back to work! You new guys can stay in the kitchen first and make some pizzas!" one of my co-workers said.

All five of them nodded silently and did their job as quietly and efficiently as they could.

The whole day passed by without any incident, which was totally surprising for me. I actually thought that those five dudes would start some kind of trouble or something. But apparently they didn't.

Maybe Jonesy was right... maybe they were actually a bunch of cool dudes once I got to know them.

But I still wanted to know where they came from at the very least. They owed us an explanation as to why all five of them suddenly came bursting through the employment door!

"I guess that's a wrap, huh Noob?" Jonesy said as he took off his Work at a Pizza Place hat and hung it on the door.

"Yeah. Pretty quiet day, considering we had five new dudes working with us!"

"See? I told you! Those guys probably aren't as bad as you might have thought. Try not to give them a hard time. Christmas is fast approaching, so don't be a grouch, dude! I'll see you tomorrow, alright?" Jonesy said.

"Yeah dude... I guess you're right. Take care now!" I told him as he waved at me and made his way towards the exit.

The five new employees were still packing up their stuff and getting ready to call it day. They obviously weren't used to the whole work schedule yet, so it took them a little bit longer than everyone else to finish cleaning everything up before going home. I knew that this was the perfect opportunity to try and get to know some of them better, so I went over to one of them and said hi.

"Hey dude! What's up?" I said to one of them.

The big dude was washing the last of the dirty plates when he suddenly noticed me walking up to him and trying to start a conversation with him. He slowly turned his head towards me and stared at me like he was going to strangle me or something. That was actually one of the scariest moments of my life! I really thought he was going to hurt me or something.

"Huh? You talkin' to me?" he said softly.

I felt like my heart just jumped out of my chest. I suddenly felt a huge wave of relief overcome my entire body. I guess he wasn't going to hurt me after all.

"Uh... yeah! I noticed that you're one of the new workers at the pizza restaurant. What's up?" I told him calmly.

"Nothing much, little dude. Just finishing up

cleaning these dishes... then I'm gonna head home afterwards. Gotta make sure I get back home soon because my wife wants me to help decorate our house for the Christmas season." he said in a nice tone of voice.

I guess Jonesy was right. These guys weren't that bad after all! This big dude seemed pretty harmless!

"Oh, cool! You're decorating your house for the Christmas season? So am I! I'm trying to think of some cool way of bringing the Christmas season to my house, but I want it to be awesome and unique at the same time... like maybe some kind of Santa Claus poster with him on it holding an electric guitar instead of a bag of presents. What do you think?"

The large dude let out a friendly laugh. He looked at me with his scary looking eyes and flashed a warm smile. He may have looked really dangerous, but I had a feeling that he wasn't all bad.

"You're funny, you know that kid? What's your name?" he asked me.

"I'm Noob! I'm also kinda new to the pizza place... I just got here a few months ago... but man, I am totally having the time of my life! It's super awesome working here in the pizza place! I'm telling you dude... you are gonna love it here! That's a promise! There's so much awesome stuff to do!"

"Is that so?"

"Yeah! You can just explore the neighborhood on weekends or party your pants off in Party Island, or you could choose to just relax at your crib! Then on weekdays, you can pick between being the cashier, the delivery guy, or the cook! I personally prefer being the delivery guy most of the time since you get to explore the entire city while handing out the pizzas!" I said excitedly.

"Seems like I made the right choice to move here then..." he said.

I looked up at the big dude and tilted my head.

"Yeah, about that... I was actually going to ask you where you were from... we haven't seen that many new workers here before."

He stopped cleaning the dishes and looked down on the floor. He let out a deep sigh and shook his head. It was as if he was hiding something deep in his heart. He looked really sad and troubled about whatever it was he was hiding too.

"I'd rather not say who I am kid... you'd probably just get away from you if I did." he said softly.

"Aw, come on dude! You can trust me! I'm Noob! Everyone trusts me! I'm the friendliest dude back in Robloxia! I won't bite, I promise."

"Alright, fine… but only because you're insisted. My name is Rojack, and this is what I used to do…"

Entry # 3:

A Blast From Rojack's Past!

"Get your butt in there Jackson! Go, go, go!" Lombard said.

Lombard was my one of my closest friends. We became friends while both of us were in prison and we kept our friendship even outside those stoney walls. The other guys in the group were just acquaintances. I didn't exactly like anyone in the group except for Lombard. He was honestly the only guy I could trust.

"Alright, dude!" Jackson said as he jumped out of the getaway car and ran straight for the back door of the bank.

Jackson was another robber just like us although I didn't really know much about him. All I knew was that he just loved to cause all sorts of trouble wherever he went.

It was a nice, sunny day at the bank of Robloxus in the Jailbreak server. Unfortunately, that day was about to get much worse for it's customers and employees when all five of us were about to rob the bank totally empty.

The five of us, all former prisoners from Jailbreak.

All of us managed to escape the prison we were all confined in when a big riot suddenly broke out inside the prison several years ago.

In all of the chaos, we managed to slip out unnoticed...

And we've been robbing banks ever since.

It was a fun life...

A dangerous life full of risks, but still fun.

"Alright, Lom! I'm going in!" I said as I jumped out of our large getaway car as well with a machine gun in my hand and pointed it straight at the security guard.

"Better not do anything funny, mister!" I shouted out.

The security guard raised his hands up in fear and all of the other robbers jumped out of the large car with their high powered assault rifles ready to shoot at a moment's notice. All of them stormed the bank with their large weapons and started pointing their guns wildly at anyone who wouldn't cooperate with them.

"All right, everyone! Listen up! We ain't here to hurt nobody! But if anyone here tries to be a hero... we ain't gonna hesitate to bury that person in lead either! So this is gonna be like a normal bank transaction! You guys hand over all the money, and nobody gets hurt. That darn simple." Lombard said.

"You're not gonna get away with this!" the bank manager said.

"Oh I think we will, mister manager! Now hand over all of the money in the bank and place them in two large handbags! Once you do that, we'll be on our way!" Lombard shouted.

"And nobody better think about pulling that alarm!" Conard said.

Conard was Lombard's right hand man. He was probably the craziest in the group too. Conard and I didn't exactly see eye to eye, but we respected each other enough to be able to work well as a team.

The manager shook his head in fear and

frustration. He gestured his hand towards one of the bank employees to bring in the bags of money that Lombard was demanding. I was still outside though, keeping watch just in case some crazy cops start showing up out of nowhere.

After a few tense and silent minutes inside the bank, the bank employee eventually came back up with two large bags full of green bank notes. We had hit the jackpot once again.

"Oh yeah, baby!" Conard said.

"Come on everyone! Let's move! Jackson! Grab one of those bags and toss the other towards me! It's time to get out of here, fast!" Lombard said.

Jackson was waiting in the back door the entire time, watching the whole thing unfold like a hawk. He suddenly sprung out from the shadows like an assassin and quickly took both of the bags away from the bank employee. He tossed one of the bags over to Lombard and the entire group began making their way towards the exit.

"Rojack! We got the money! Let's make a break for it!" Lombard said.

Just as soon as the whole group had their feet outside of the bank, we suddenly heard the sound of the bank's alarm blaring all throughout the whole area. It was a defeaning sound that my ears had gotten used to after robbing so many banks. The whole group and I instantly knew that the cops would be here any minute, so we had to get to the getaway car as quickly as possible.

Our getaway driver, Cobra, was anxiously waiting for us inside the large SUV car that was just parked around the bank.

"Where are those guys?!" Cobra asked himself quietly as he looked around inside his vehicle.

All four of us started running towards the getaway car as quickly as we could, although we weren't really sure we were going to make it. We could already here several sirens in the distance, and those cops are a lot faster than you might think!

Luckily for us though, Cobra himself drove over to where we were. He lowered the window on the SUV and gestured his hand for us to come inside the car.

"Get in, quick!" he said.

"Ya don't need to tell us twice!" Lombard said.

Everyone jumped inside the vehicle like a bunch of clowns who were stuffing themselves inside a small car. There were bank notes flying everywhere from the money bags that Jackson and Lombard were carrying too. It was a chaotic scene, and we could already see a group of police vehicles closing in on the bank.

"Step on it, Cobra! Step on it!" Lombard shouted out.

Cobra nodded his head and stepped on the SUV's gas pedal as hard as he could. The car's engine roared to life and it sped away onto the narrow side streets of the city away from the bank. The cops arrived only after we were long gone from the scene. The policemen wanted to chase after us and make a perimeter surrounding the whole place, but they knew it was going to be difficult. We had already gotten pretty far, and everyone knew that we had it in the bag.

"Oh yeah! We did it guys! We did it again! Too easy!" Lombard said excitedly. He pumped his fist up in the air and so did everyone else.

"Easy! Let's split the money fairly once we

reach the boss' place later." Cobra said.

"When's the next robbery gonna be? Those cops are getting sloppier and sloppier each time we do this! They've gotta up their game!" Conard said as he shook his head in disappointment.

I wasn't exactly sure why he wanted the cops to improve in any way. I was just happy that we had always gotten away somehow after each bank robbery we attempted. Wasn't that the whole point in the first place? To rob the bank and not get caught?

"Hey, let's just be happy that we're still not in prison, alright? Any other normal group would have been behind bars for a long time now after doing what we've done, but somehow, the cops just haven't found a way to catch us yet." I said.

"Well they should! I agree with Conard. They're makin' this too easy! They gotta make it fun!" Jackson said.

I shook my head and let out a deep sigh. Robbing banks wasn't about having fun! It was about getting the money! You can have all the fun you want later when you get your share of the money! Jackson and Conard were just crazy.

"Look guys, we did it! Let's just make it back to the boss' place." Cobra said as he calmly drove the car towards the big boss' giant palace.

The big boss.

Darn... I hated dealing with that guy.

Sure, he was the reason all of us were out of prison in the first place...

He was the one who made that riot happen in the Jailbreak Inmate Housing Facility!

Still...

He was a real jerk.

And I knew that everyone within the group agreed with me. Nobody wanted to deal with the big boss! He always took most of the money from our robberies even though he never even showed up to a single one!

And the worst part was...

We didn't even know what his name actually was!

He was known to us and everyone else only as the "Christmas Grouch".

He was a grouchy dude alright, and he didn't seem to like Christmas at all... Which was pretty weird, considering everyone loved Christmas! Even robbers like us take a break from robbing banks to chill out with our friends and family.

He was the only person I knew that disliked Christmas for some strange reason.

I wonder why..?

"Yeah.. let's just make it over to the boss' place. We got what we wanted now, didn't we guys?" Lombard said.

Lombard was the head of our little group, but even he knew that the Christmas Grouch was our ultimate boss. Everyone in the group, including him, had to answer to the Christmas Grouch.

Everyone inside the SUV nodded their heads in agreement. Nobody wanted to say it, but everyone knew that the Christmas Grouch was a real jerk... even amongst bank robbers!

But that was what we did to earn a living. We had no other choice. That was the only thing we knew... to rob a bunch of banks and walk away with a ton of cash from their big vaults.

Our life continued on like this for what felt like several decades...

Until we finally thought enough was enough. It was time for a new life.

So all of us eventually agreed on living a normal life, working as a normal person in a normal job.

And what better place to do that than the Work at a Pizza Place server, right?

Entry # 4:

The Beginning Of A New Friendship.

My eyes widened at Rojack's crazy story. I knew he looked big, mean and scary and all... but I would have never thought that he was a bank robber before!

"Whoah, whoah, whoah! So you were actually a criminal before you came to work here?" I asked him.

"Yep. But don't get the wrong idea though, kid! I never hurt anybody. Sure, I went inside those banks with giant guns and stuff, but I never shot anyone with those guns! That was never my intention! I just wanted the money, you know?" Rojack said.

"Yeah, I feel you... sometimes, I feel like just bursting through Santy's door and demanding for a big raise! But I know he isn't gonna give it to me just yet... maybe someday though."

Rojack let out a soft chuckle.

"Yeah... that's just life, huh? Well, that's it. Now you know... who I am, where I came from, and who those other four guys are. We all used to rob banks at Jailbreak... then we just kinda thought it was time to start a new life, work at a normal place like all the other normal people." he said.

"But are you guys happy with your decision? I mean, don't you ever feel like you wanna go back to robbing banks someday?"

Rojack shook his head slowly and sighed.

"You know kid, those thoughts do kinda enter my mind sometimes... but I can't do that stuff no more. I've already done enough bad things... it was time for me to start living a normal life. And besides, I don't wanna go back to prison anyways. Sure, I miss the adrenaline, the rush of going into a bank and getting away from the cops... those were sure crazy times. But I'm getting' old, ya hear? I gotta lie low, just relax."

"Hey, I feel you dude! Trust me, I do! I've fought in countless battles before with some of the nastiest people in Roblox! I've even fought giant monsters, squids, disciplined martial arts masters, conquerors, you name it!"

Rojack gave me a look of confusion and scratched his head. He wasn't really sure if I was joking or if I was actually being serious.

"Uh... yeah... wow."

"But that's why I moved here to the Work at a Pizza Place server! All that crazy fighting and stuff kinda made me look for a normal life, just like you! It was just getting way out of hand."

Rojack let out a friendly laugh and smiled at me as he wrapped his huge arm around my shoulder.

"Hey, I like you, kid. I like your style. You're real cool. I'm glad you and I met here."

"I feel the same way, Rojack! Hey, you wanna swing by my place later and play some video games? I'm also gonna be decorating the house since Christmas is just around the corner!"

Rojack shook his head and picked up what looked like a small backpack in the kitchen.

"Nah, kid... I gotta go back to my place and rest. It's been a long day. Thanks for the offer though. I'll see you back here in the pizza place tomorrow, yeah?"

"For sure, Rojack! You take care now!"

Rojack and I waved at each other before parting ways.

I guess Jonesy was right after all! Sure, those guys were bank robbers before they came here at the Work at a Pizza Place server, but you can't judge them because of that! I did a lot of crazy things too before I got to this server! Rojack was a pretty nice guy and he wanted to settle down in this server, and I totally understood where he was coming from.

In the end, everything turned out okay.

The five new dudes I was so worried about turned out to be a bunch of harmless people who just wanted to live normal lives, and Christmas was still fast approaching!

There were a lot of cool stuff to look forward to!

Yeah, everything was going great...

Well, until "it" happened.

What is "it", you may ask?

Read on, my friend... and you'll find out soon enough!

Entry # 5:

Santy's Request!

"Good morning, Work at a Pizza Place server!" I said as I jumped out of my bed and put on my threads for the day.

The day started off just like any other, with me doing my usual routine of brushing up, doing a bit of cleaning and making my way to work over at the pizza restaurant.

Yeah, everything was pretty normal that day and nothing was out of whack.

Well, that is, at least until I finally got to the restaurant.

When I had finally got there, the main doors to the pizza parlor were mysteriously closed!

I was pretty sure that the pizza restaurant was already open at this time, and nobody told me about any holidays on that day. Christmas was still a good couple of weeks away, and there was just no reason to close the restaurant down!

The main doors also had yellow police tape all over them that read "POLICE: DO NOT CROSS:".

Something very weird and unusual was going on...

"Whoah, whoah, whoah! What's going on here?" I asked myself as I struggled to make sense of what was going on.

Jonesy arrived just a few minutes after me and he looked like he had no idea on what was going on either.

"Dude! Why's the restaurant closed? Did we get a day off?" he asked me.

"No, man… Santy would have told us if the restaurant was going to close! Something's going on here! And look! There's some kind of police tape all over the main entrance!"

Jonesy leaned in closer to inspect the police tape and shook his head slowly. He knew that something was off too.

"Whoah… this looks serious… what happened? Maybe those five dudes had something to do with this?" Jonesy said.

And that's when it hit me.

The five new guys!

The former bank robbers!

They must have done something terrible!

But why would they do that? I had a good talk with Rojack last night and he seemed really sincere about turning a new leaf! It just didn't make any sense as to why he'd throw all that away just to commit some kind of weird crime!

"Yeah... those five dudes probably have something to do with this. They were former bank robbers after all, you know." I told Jonesy.

"W-what?! Former bank robbers?! Now how'd you know that?"

"I talked to one of them, Rojack. He seemed like a pretty cool guy! He told me all about his crazy robberies back in the Jailbreak server. But it just doesn't make any sense! He's already tired of his life of crime! Why would he ever want to go back? That's the reason why he went to this server in the first place! To just chill out and live a normal life away from all the crime!"

"Maybe he and his friends came here so they

could rob some banks in this server?" Jonesy speculated.

I shook my head and sighed. I was pretty sure that Rojack was a good guy. I couldn't imagine him going back to his bank robbing ways. But what about his friends though? Maybe they were the ones who did it... whatever the crime was in the first place!

"We have to go in, dude! We gotta know what happened!" I told Jonesy.

Jonesy gave me a weird look of disbelief on his face.

"Dude! Are you kidding me? It says DO NOT ENTER! We're not supposed to go inside! Who knows what we're going to see? And besides, the police might even arrest us for going in there! I dunno about you, but I think I just wanna chill out a Party Island for now until this whole thing is over." Jonesy said.

"Oh come on, Jonesy! This is where we work! We have a right to know what's going on! We've gotta get inside somehow! You know this won't fix itself, and we gotta get to the bottom of this!" I insisted.

Jonesy let out a deep sigh and shook his head.

"You just don't give up, do you, Noob?"

"Of course not! We have to know what's going on, dude! Come on!" I said.

"Well, at least take the back door! It sure doesn't look like it's wrapped in all sorts of crazy tape!" Jonesy said.

I turned my head over to the back door of the restaurant and noticed that wasn't wrapped in the same police tape that the main entrance was all taped up with. Jonesy was right! It would probably be the smarter decision to go through the back instead.

"Alright dude. Let's go through the back!"

Jonesy nodded his head and followed me as I slowly walked over to the back door of the restaurant. I gently opened the door and peeked inside. The whole place seemed completely untouched and everything looked pretty normal...

Except for the fact that there were three police officers at the customer area near the main entrance. I caught a glimpse of Santy who was talking with one of the officers inside the place too.

"You see that, dude? There are cops in there!" Jonesy whispered.

"Yeah, but why? Let's go ask Santy!" I said just before I walked through the back door.

"N-no, Noob wait up--"

Jonesy wasn't even able to finish what he was saying before I busted through the restaurant's back door. All of the officers quickly turned their heads towards me and so did Santy. All of them looked surprised to see someone like me walking into the whole crime scene.

"Who are you?" one of the officers said.

"That's Noob! He's one of my employees! I don't think he knows about what happened yet!" Santy said.

"Yeah, Santy! I was gonna ask you about this whole thing! Why is the main entrance closed? And when are we going to work?"

"Sorry Noob... but there isn't going to be any work today. Something terrible just happened!" Santy said.

"What do you mean by that?" I asked him.

"Well, two of our newest employees to the restaurant have just been killed! That and one of our oldest workers, Jay, was murdered too! It's just awful!"

My eyes widened at Santy and I suddenly felt nauseous. I wasn't sure how take in what Santy had just told me. Everything was going great when I first got into the Work at a Pizza Place server... and now, all of a sudden, this?!

A string of mysterious murders in a peaceful server like this?

I wasn't really sure how to take it in.

"W-what..? Are you serious, Santy?" I asked him.

I knew that Jonesy was just behind me and that he had heard every single word that Santy just said. He was pretty speechless, and I was sure that he couldn't believe any of it too.

"Yes! Christmas is going to get ruined because of this! Someone needs to get to the bottom of this whole thing!" Santy said.

"Don't worry about it, Mr. Santy. We'll catch the villain who committed these awful crimes!" one of the police officers said.

"I'm sure you will, officer. Could I talk to Noob privately for a few moments in my office though, officer?" Santy said.

I leaned back in surprise at Santy's request. Why would he want to talk to me of all people? Did he suspect that I had something to do with the crime? I was innocent, I tell ya! I had nothing to do with any of that stuff! I just got to the pizza place!

"W-why would you wanna talk to me, Santy?" I asked him.

"It's something private, Noob. Officer?"

"Yes, of course, sir. Take your time." the police officer said before he knelt down and inspected the entire scene of the crime.

Santy gestured his hand towards me, telling

me to come with him inside his office. I could feel my heart starting to jump out of it's chest again as I slowly walked in. I knew in my heart that I was innocent, but what if they were going to try and put the blame on me or something? This was getting crazy!

I gently shut the door behind us.I could hear every single screw and hinge working inside the door as it slowly closed itself onto the lock. The tension in the air was so great, you could almost cut it with a knife!

"Noob--"

"Look, dude, Santy, before you say anything, I swear, I didn't do it! I didn't do anything! I didn't even know that someone was actually murdered! I swear, I just got here! Look, don't put the blame on me, I know in my heart I'm innocent--"

"Noob, let me speak--"

"Santy, you can't put the blame on me, dude! I didn't have anything to do with it!"

Santy let out a deep sigh as he shook his head.

"I'm not trying to blame you for anything!" Santy snapped.

I leaned back in surprise at Santy's sudden burst of anger.

"Wait... you're not?"

"Of course not! Why would I ever blame you for this whole thing? I know you, Noob! You'd never hurt a fly!" Santy said.

"So wait... then if you're not blaming me for the whole thing, then why did you want to talk to me privately in your office?" I asked him bluntly.

Santy let out a deep sigh again before he slowly took a seat onto his plush, leather chair.

"I need your help, Noob." he said as he leaned forward with his hands clasped together.

"You need my help? For what?"

"I need you to investigate this whole crime for me! You need to find out who the real killer is before Christmas!"

I gave my manager a confused look. Was he serious? Why was he asking my help to find the real killer? I don't know anything about being a detective!

"Wait... you're kidding, right?" I said.

"I'm afraid not. You're going to have to investigate this whole crime!"

"Why me? Isn't that the police's job?"

"Those guys are unreliable! They won't be able to find the killer in time. They've got too many cases to work on, and this thing will go on way past Christmas! We need to resolve this case as soon as possible! If not, Christmas will get ruined for not only the entire restaurant, but the entire server as well! It's terrible!"

"Okay, I understood the part where you said that it would ruin Christmas for the restaurant... but for the whole server? Come on!" I protested.

Santy sneered at me and shook his head.

"Oh, come on Noob! Think about it! This is the only place in the entire server where people get their pizza! And this game is, after all, called 'Work at a Pizza Place', so if this pizza restaurant goes down, then everyone else's Christmas is ruined! No killer, no pizza, no restaurant, no Christmas! ... And no pizza!" Santy said.

I looked up at the ceiling and thought about Santy's argument. I guess he was right. This place really was the only restaurant that dished out pizzas. Without the restaurant, there would be no pizzas! And that would mean that Christmas would be ruined for everyone!

"Wait... I still don't understand why you would pick me to investigate though. How was I supposed to find this killer? Why not Jonesy?" I asked him.

"I remember it said somewhere in your resume when you first applied for a job here at the restaurant that you spent some time in the Murder Mystery 2 server! That means you have experience in finding out about murders!"

I shook my head in disagreement and sighed. I honestly didn't even want to recall what happened over there when I was at the Murder Mystery 2 server. It was just terrible.

"Look, Santy... I know where you're coming

from... But I can't just solve this case on my own! That's the whole reason I went over to this server from the Murder Mystery 2 server! I wanted to get away from it all! You're better off hiring a private investigator on this matter or something."

"Noob, please! You have to help! Think about all of the customers! Think about Christmas!"

I shook my head one more time and let out a deep sigh.

"I'm sorry, Santy. I just can't do it."

I didn't even stick around to hear what else Santy had to say as I immediately left his office afterwards. I headed straight home towards my new crib and thought about the whole incident the entire day.

Who was the killer?

Why did he kill those former robbers and even that innocent pizza employee?

What were his motives behind killing them?

So many questions...

And no anwers.

But I guess that wasn't supposed to be my job, right?

That was the police's job... or a detective's job.

Not mine. I was just an ordinary pizza restaurant employee.

I did my best to shrug off everything that was in my mind that day.

"I'd better not think about this whole thing. I bet it'll all just be over a few days later! Yeah... it's all going to go back to normal."

Little did I know that this was actually just the beginning.

Entry # 6:

Solving The Unsolvable Case!

A few short, uneventful days passed since that crazy incident at the pizza restaurant. Santy told all of his employees through text message to take a couple of days off before going back to work because of the incident. I decided to take one extra day off from work just to be sure that things are back to normal.

The day finally arrived when it was time to go back to work at the pizza place, and I was hoping that things would go back to the way they were...

But apparently, it only got worse.

The image that met my eyes was a familiar one: the main entrance was closed down yet again and wrapped up in yellow colored police tape. The whole restaurant felt like a barren wasteland with no customers to be found anywhere. I walked over to the back door which was the same place I entered when I first saw the restaurant in this state.

Once inside, I saw Santy talking to the same officers I saw him talking to a couple of days ago.

"Santy?! I thought the restaurant was open yesterday? Why is it still closed?" I asked him.

"Yet another string of murders occurred yesterday, Noob! Just when everyone thought that everything was going to go back to normal, a few more murders happened again! Cammy and Cecille were the ones who were killed this time! This is terrible! Christmas is definitely going to be ruined now! I can't believe this is happening to us!" Santy said in a frenzied panic.

I couldn't believe what I was hearing.

Two more murders?

This was getting way out of hand!

Maybe Santy was right...

I wasn't just about to stand around while this crazy murderer was on the loose!

I had to somehow find a way!

For all the people this monster has killed...

For Christmas!

"Uhh... Santy... could you and I talk again privately in your office? I have something I need to tell you." I said.

Santy's face suddenly changed. He seemed genuinely confused by my strange request. I had already turned down his request to find the killer in our previous private talk inside his office, so I guess he wasn't sure what I had wanted this time around.

"Uh... Okay. Sure thing, Noob. Officers?"

"Yes sir. Take your time." one of the officers said as he was once again inspecting the scene of the crime.

Santy and I walked over to his private quarters and I waited for him to sit down before I closed the door behind us.

"So what do you want, Noob?" Santy asked me bluntly.

I was surprised by Santy's direct question. I thought he would have wanted to ask me to investigate the matter one more time. I guess he's already decided to go in it alone even if it destroys Christmas for the entire server. Fortunately for him, I'm not about to let that happen anymore!

"Santy... I thought about your request."

"Request? What request?"

"The one where you asked me to investigate this case and to find the real killer of those people!"

Santy nodded his head slowly.

"Oh... that. Well, didn't you already tell me before that you weren't interested in finding out who it was?"

"Well, I did a lot of thinking, and after seeing two more people get killed, I guess I figured that I can't just stand around and do nothing. I can't let Christmas get ruined not only for the restaurant but for the entire server as well just because of this maniac! We gotta catch him! I'll do it, Santy! I'm going to find this killer before those cops do... and before Christmas!"

Santy's eyes widened after hearing what I

had just said. I saw a faint glimmer of hope in his eyes, and I could tell that he was really happy to hear me accept his request.

"Wow... that's great to hear, Noob! Finally! Now do you see why this is so important?"

"Yeah... I see that now. We're gonna catch this killer, Santy! Don't you worry!"

"It's gonna be just like the time you were at the Murder Mystery 2 server! Only it's taking place here at the Work at a Pizza Place server! Weird, huh?"

I shook my head again and sighed. I really didn't want to recall what had happened there in my time at the Murder Mystery 2 server. I remember something terrible happened there... in fact, it was so darn terrible that I had completely forgot about it!

"Yeah... I guess so. I'd better start on that investigation right away, Santy."

Santy nodded his head and smiled.

"Hey, if you need any help, I'll be here."

"Actually... about that. I think I'm going to need your help right about now." I said.

"Shoot! What is it?"

"You said that two of the new employees were killed just a few days ago, right? Who were they?"

"Cobra and Conard were the ones that got killed. Rojack, Jackson and Lombard showed up for work this morning, and then suddenly, this happened again."

I nodded my head as I listened to Santy's every word.

"Are you aware that those guys used to be robbers before they got a job here at the pizza restaurant?" I said.

Santy leaned back in surprise and his eyes

widened after hearing my last remark. It was pretty obvious that he had no idea about their past.

"W-what?! Are you serious?"

"Yeah! One of them just told me about their history! Rojack!"

Santy looked down on the floor and crossed his arms.

"Oh no... then that must mean that they probably had something to do with this crime!"

"Exactly! I'm going to need their addresses, Santy. I think I'm going to pay one of them a visit... see what they know about this whole thing."

"Of course, of course! Just give me a few moments to get their resumes..." Santy said before he pulled up one of his drawers and reached out for a stack of papers piled on top of one another.

"These are their resumes. They should have their addresses listed on each of them." Santy said as he handed me the papers.

I carefully observed each piece of paper and found the addresses of the three remaining former bank robbers: Rojack, Lombard and Jackson.

"All right... thanks Santy. I think someone's gonna pay these dudes a visit pretty soon... and it's probably not going to be Santa Claus." I said.

Entry # 7:

Meeting Lombard The (Former) Robber!

It was a long walk over to Lombard's place. I didn't expect him to live so far away from the pizza restaurant, but I thought that he was the best person to talk to when it came to this crazy crime. After all, Rojack mentioned before that he was the head of the group, second only to the Christmas Grouch. That must have meant that he knew the Christmas Grouch better than anyone else did, and something in my gut told me that the Christmas Grouch had something to do with all of these murders.

Lombard's house was nothing but a small, white, plain bungalow located in the middle of a quiet suburb. You could never have guessed that the person living inside it actually used to rob banks for a living.

I knocked on the door gently in order to see if he was inside. I heard a few footsteps coming from inside the house shortly afterward, and a large, scary looking dude who looked just like Rojack suddenly came to greet me at the front door.

"Uh... who are you?" he asked me.

"I'm Noob.... from the pizza place! I'm one of your co-workers!" I said.

He nodded his head slowly in acknowledgement.

"Oh... yeah. I remember you. I saw you talking to Rojack the other day. What's up?" he asked me casually.

"Yeah... I was kind of here to ask you a few questions about the murders that have been going on at the pizza restaurant."

Lombard shook his head quickly and sneered at me.

"Hey, look kid... if you think I'm the one who did those murders, then you're wrong. I'm guessing Rojack already told you that we used to be bank robbers, but rest assured that we've never actually murdered anyone before. That's just not our style. We only robbed banks because we needed the money, not because we wanted to kill anybody." Lombard said.

"I know, I know... yeah, he already told me that. I'm not here because I think you did it. I wanted to ask you why you guys stopped robbing banks... that and I wanted to know more about your big boss. Well, your former big boss, actually."

"The former big boss? You mean the Christmas Grouch?" he said.

"Yeah! That's the guy! I wanted to ask you some questions about him too."

"Why is that? Are you some kind of cop or something?" he asked defensively.

I raised one of my eyebrows and Lombard and looked at him sternly.

"Uh... why? Would it matter to you if I was?"

"Yeah, because if you're here to arrest me because of all the bank robberies I did back in Jailbreak, then forget it! I ain't going back to jail!" he cried out.

"Whoah, whoah, whoah, dude! Calm down! I'm not a cop. I'm more of a private investigator, actually. I'm not really interested in your bank robberies back in the Jailbreak server... I'm only here to solve the case that's happening right now."

Lombard let out a deep sigh and gestured his arm for me to come in.

"Fine. Come on in, kid. Let's hear those questions."

I clasped my hands together in excitement as I walked inside Lombard's quaint, little house. My plan had worked, and I was one step closer to finding the truth and closing this case. Lombard's knowledge would undoubtedly help me in solving this case for good!

"Sit down over there, kid. You want some coffee?" Lombard asked me.

Lombard pointed towards what looked like a small, leather couch in the middle of his living room. The interior of his house was surprisingly big, considering the house itself looked so small from the outside. I was also pretty surprised at Lombard's offer for some coffee, but I wasn't here to sip some hot mocha now, was I? No... I was here to solve a case!

"No thanks, Lombard." I said as I plopped my rear down on his small, leather couch.

Lombard repeated the gesture as he sat on a small, wooden chair across the couch I was sitting on.

"All right, Noob. What do you wanna know?" he asked me.

"Well... first of all, I actually wanted to know why you guys stopped robbing banks. I mean, it actually sounded like you guys were making a lot of money... so why'd you guys quit?"

"Pretty sure Rojack already told you the answer to that." he said.

"Yeah... he said he wanted to live a normal life and that he didn't want to go to jail."

Lombard let out a soft chuckle as he shook his head slowly.

"It was never really that simple, kid…"

"What do you mean?" I asked Lombard eagerly.

"Allow me to explain…"

Entry # 8:

A Blast From The Past Part Two: Lombard's Story!

The air was cold and thick inside the big boss' office. The big boss himself lived inside some kind of white marble mansion in the middle of a secret, undisclosed location somewhere in Jailbreak. Only all five of us knew where he lived, and all of us swore to never reveal his location to anyone else.

The big boss was waiting for the five of us inside his office, just as we had expected. We had just successfully robbed another bank, and it was time for us to split the money.

"Here you go, boss. Ten million Robux from the bank." Jackson said as he plopped the two large bags of money onto the big boss' desk. The big boss himself had his back turned away from us as he was sitting in his large, executive style leather chair.

"Good work, boys." he said in a really deep and creepy voice.

"So how we gonna split this one, boss? You agreed to a bigger split the last time..." Rojack said softly.

The big boss suddenly turned around to face us. He was wearing his usual ten thousand robux suit while he was smoking one of his trademark cigars. His eyes peered straight through Rojack's body, and he didn't look happy at all after hearing what Rojack had just said.

"9.5 million Robux for me. One hundred thousand Robux for each of you." he said sternly.

Everyone in the room raised their hands in disapproval.

"Oh, come on, boss! You said you'd give us a pretty big share this time! You get all the money whenever we split on these robberies!" Jackson protested.

"Yeah! And besides... you don't even show up to help us in the robberies! We're the ones who go out there and put our butts on the line!" I said firmly.

Everyone in the room stared at me strangely, like they had just seen a ghost or something. Nobody expected me to say something like that to the boss, since everyone in the group totally feared the Christmas Grouch. In fact, everyone in the entire Jailbreak server knew who the Christmas Grouch was, and no one dared to ever cross him in anything!

The boss turned his attention towards me and his eyes stared straight at mine. It was an extremely tense moment, and everyone in the room stayed quiet like a pack of gargoyle statues waiting outside a dark mansion.

"What did you just say to me..?" he said.

"You heard me! We put our butts on the line out there! We could get shot by the police! Get busted in handcuffs! Tossed into prison! Beat up by bystanders and security guards! All you do is sit around in your leather chair, barking out orders, and for some reason, you get all the loot! It's not fair!" I shouted out.

This was the first time that anyone has ever stood up to the Christmas Grouch. I caught a glimpse of Rojack staring at me, and he couldn't believe what was coming out of my lips. I always knew that Rojack himself never liked the big boss, but he never really could say what he felt since he was just too afraid of him.

The big boss' fists clenched together in anger, and his eyebrows raised in the heat of his fiery anger.

"You... dare to speak back at me?!" the big boss said.

"Hey, look boss... no offense, but Lombard's right! You did agree to give us a bigger split this time around! Why are we getting the same rate as last time?" Rojack said.

"That's none of your business! Plans change! I'm the boss here and I'll do whatever I please! So all of you shut up and take your darn money! Either that or all of you are going to end up back in your respective prison cells! You dumb-dumbs had better not forget that I was the one who got you out! I was the reason why that riot happened, and I am the reason all of you are in here in my office, robbing banks! Don't you ever forget that!" he said angrily.

That was it.

I just couldn't take it anymore.

I could take him treating us like garbage...

Or him taking most of the money from the robbery...

But he lied. He said he'd give us a bigger split that time around.

He lied, and he clearly doesn't care about us.

"That's it. I don't care anymore. I don't care if you were the one who set us free. You clearly don't care about us! This is crazy! I quit!" I said as stormed out of the Christmas Grouch's office.

He quickly stood up from his executive style leather chair and pointed his finger straight at me.

"Hey! Where do you think you're going?! Get

back here!" he shouted.

The rest of the gang shook their heads slowly and followed my example. All of us left the boss' office one by one, and soon enough, he was all alone. We had had enough.

If we were going to rob banks, then we were going to do it for ourselves. We didn't need the Christmas Grouch to back us up for anything. All he wanted was to take advantage of us anyway!

I felt someone grab on to my shoulder as I continued to walk away from the Christmas Grouch's large, marble mansion.

It was Rojack.

"Hey, Lom... Took a lot of guts to say and do what you did back there." he said.

I nodded my head slowly and smiled at my friend.

"Hey... he was takin' advantage of us now, wasn't he?"

"Course he was! We're free men now. Ain't no jerk gonna tie us down anymore!" Rojack said happily.

"Do you think the big boss is gonna get back at us somehow?" I asked him nervously.

"Nah. And besides... don't call him that anymore. He ain't our big boss anymore. This time... We're the bosses now." Rojack said.

I shook Rojack's hand in agreement, and I thought that everything had ended well. I thought that we had a bright future ahead of us since we were now free from the Christmas Grouch. We were free to do what we wanted, when we wanted without some kind of boss always telling us what to do.

Apparently, I was wrong.

Let's just say that the Christmas Grouch didn't

exactly like what I had told him that day, and all of us felt it in the days that followed.

Rojack himself suddenly disappeared without a trace for a few days and nobody really knew why. When we he finally returned, we asked him where we went off to but he never really told us the real reason why he disappeared in the first place. He'd always just keep quiet whenever we would ask him about that.

Shortly afterwards, we also tried robbing a few more banks after that incident, but we noticed that for some reason, the cops knew exactly when and where we were going to rob a bank. We always left the banks we were going to rob empty handed, and we were losing money fast.

Rojack disappearing for a few days...

The cops knowing exactly when and where we were going to rob banks...

All of us losing money with each passing second...

They weren't just mere coincidences. I knew that the Christmas Grouch had something to do with all of that stuff.

So the five of us simply decided that it wasn't safe to rob banks anymore. We had to get away from Jailbreak... away from the Christmas Grouch.

Entry # 9:

The Prime Suspect!

"And so here we are. All five of us agreed that this would be the perfect place to hide from the Christmas Grouch... but apparently, I guess we were wrong again, huh?" Lombard said.

"Whoah... that's a crazy story! But tell me, Lombard... do you know anything else about the Christmas Grouch other than the fact that he's a really rich, criminal boss?" I asked Lombard.

"Well, now that you asked, yeah... I hear that he's got the ability to change skins whenever he wants since he's so rich. You never really know if you're talking to the Christmas Grouch because he could just be someone you know in disguise!" Lombard said before he suddenly stared at me with his big scary eyes.

"Wait a minute... you're not the Christmas Grouch now, are you?" he suddenly asked me.

I leaned back in surprise at Lombard's strange question.

"Of course not! Why would I be?! I'm trying to ask you about the Christmas Grouch, so that wouldn't make any sense now, would it? I mean, if I was really the Christmas Grouch, would I be asking you a bunch of questions about myself?" I told him bluntly.

Lombard suddenly scratched his head and looked away.

"Uh.. yeah. I guess you're right. Oh and there's another thing, by the way..."

"Yeah?"

"The Christmas Grouch sent all five of us a letter before we left Jailbreak, saying that he would ruin Christmas for all of us wherever we'd go! I guess he really did make good on that promise!" Lombard said.

I knew it!

Lombard and Rojack's Stories...

The mysterious string of murders...

And right when Christmas is about to begin...

It all makes sense now!

The Christmas Grouch must be behind this whole thing!

Which only leaves one question...

Where is he?

I needed some time to think about all of the information that I'd already gotten. I needed to somehow connect the dots in order to find the Christmas Grouch.

"I see… Well, thanks for all your help, Lombard. I'll need to get back to my crib in order to investigate this case even further. I think we're all one step closer to finding out who this killer really is and where he's hiding at!" I told him.

Lombard nodded his head and reached out his hand.

"Any time, kid." he said.

I reached out and shook Lombard's hand firmly. He was a really big help in shedding some light about this case!

After saying goodbye, I quickly made my way back to my hot crib at the Work at a Pizza Place server. I needed to connect all the dots in order to see just where the Christmas Grouch was hiding. My house was pretty far away from Lombard's place, but I managed to get there just in time. Once I had gotten home, I quickly took out some notes and began studying about all the information I'd uncovered so far.

The old robberies committed by the five robbers...

Their disagreements with the Christmas Grouch...

The Christmas' Grouch's ability to change skins and his wealth...

Lombard's rebellion against the Christmas Grouch...

Rojack's mysterious disappearance...

Their failed robberies at the Jailbreak server...

Their sudden appearance here at the Work

at a Pizza Place server...

And now, the string of mysterious murders.

Everything seemed to make sense to me except for one thing...

Why did Rojack disappear that time? Why didn't he tell his friends where he went?

I had no idea!

It just didn't make any sense!

Did he take some kind of strange vacation?

Or maybe he watched a football game with some new friends with all of the money he's stolen from the banks?

"It doesn't make sense!" I shouted out as I crumpled up one of my notes and threw the piece of paper against the wall.

After thinking about Rojack's mysterious disappearance over and over again, I unknowingly dozed off into a deep sleep right while I was sitting on my study desk.

Once I finally woke up the next day, it all finally made sense to me.

Entry # 10:

So Close, Yet So Far Away...

Rojack "disappeared" because he was actually killed by the Christmas Grouch!

And since the Christmas Grouch can easily change skins...

He must have changed his skin to match Rojack's!

And that's how the cops knew about their robberies!

He disguised himself as Rojack in order to hear where they would rob the next bank and when...

Then he disguised himself as a cop afterwards so he could let the police know about their next move!

It all made sense now!

Rojack wasn't really Rojack...

Rojack was actually the Christmas Grouch in disguise!

"I've got to tell Santy before it's too late! Rojack is actually the Christmas Grouch! He's the one who's been killing all of the people at the pizza restaurant! He wants to ruin Christmas for everyone!" I told myself.

I quickly jumped on to some new threads before bursting through the front door of my house. I ran as fast as I could towards the pizza restaurant, dodging and weaving through every person I ran across on the sidewalk.

When I had finally arrived at the pizza place,

the whole restaurant appeared to be open for business as usual. Once I went inside through the back door, there were employees hustling and bustling everywhere. It was as if nothing had ever even happened, and everyone was acting like it was just another normal day at the pizza place.

"Hey, Noob! You finally made it to work!" Jonesy said with a smile as he caught a glimpse of me standing near the back door.

"Jonesy! Where's Santy? I need to talk to him!" I said.

Jonesy suddenly gave me confused look.

"Santy? But Santy just quit his job this morning. We've got a new manager now... and all of us got a raise from the new manager!"

I wasn't sure how to take in what Jonesy just told me. A new manager?! What happened to Santy? I didn't care about the raise anymore... I just wanted to save Christmas and catch that evil Christmas Grouch!

"Dude... I don't care about that raise! Where's Santy? I just need to talk to him!" I said.

"But Noob... you've been talking about that raise all these years, and now you're telling me that you don't care about it?"

"Look, Jonesy... I'm really close to solving the murders that happened on this restaurant! But I'm going to need to talk to Santy if I want to catch the killer!"

"Well, you're out of luck dude... no one's seen Santy ever since. He just quit all of sudden. No one really knows why."

That was just impossible! It wasn't like Santy to just quit his job like that, especially not when Christmas was so close! I bet the Christmas Grouch had something to do with

Santy's disappearance.

"Fine! Could you at least tell me where Rojack and Lombard are?"

"Dude... didn't you hear about the news?" Jonesy said softly.

"What? No, I didn't."

"Lombard was murdered in his own house last night!"

I suddenly felt my heart just jump out of my chest after hearing Jonesy break the news to me. Now there was definitely no doubt that the Christmas Grouch had something to do with all of this!

"W-what..?"

"Yeah... crazy, huh?"

"D-dude, where's Rojack?! At least let me talk to him!" I pleaded.

"I dunno, Noob. He didn't show up for work

this morning. He pretty much disappeared, just like Santy. Jackson's still here, though."

I slapped my palm onto my face and sighed. I was so close to solving this case and I had already uncovered the Christmas Grouch's identity. Now it suddenly feels as if the case had gone completely cold once again.

"Darn it! That Christmas Grouch is a smart jerk!"

"The Christmas who?" Jonesy asked me.

"The Christmas Grouch! He's the one behind all of the murders! He was disguising himself as Rojack and committed all of the murders in the restaurant! He wants to ruin Christmas for everyone on this server! Now I'll never be able to find him." I said.

"The Christmas Grouch..? Well... I really have no idea what you're talking about Noob, but if you want to look for Rojack, then you might as well just wait until he shows up for work."

"He's not going to show up for work, Jonesy! He already knows that I know he's the Christmas Grouch! He's obviously covered his tracks! We're doomed! Christmas is ruined!" I said desperately.

Jonesy approached me and placed his arm around my shoulder.

"Hey, dude... Don't sweat it. Here, take your mind off this whole murder thing and just try working. Serving out some pizzas might get this whole case out of your head." Jonesy said as he handed me a white chef's hat.

It just wasn't the same.

The cops would never believe me if I went up to them and told them that my co-worker, Rojack, was actually the Christmas Grouch in disguise. It was hopeless. Christmas was going to get ruined!

I guess Jonesy was right.

If Christmas this year was going to get ruined by that jerk, the Christmas Grouch... I might as well at least enjoy working at the pizza place. What else could I have done, right? With Santy gone, there was no way anyone was going to believe me!

I slowly placed the white chef's hat onto my head and let out a deep sigh of surrender. The Christmas Grouch had won.

Or has he..?

Entry # 11:

The Case Is Back On The Table!

I had totally resigned to my fate and decided to and focus on my work instead of focusing on the case that had went cold. What was the point of thinking about catching the Christmas Grouch if Rojack and Santy were gone? No one would believe me.

I shook my head to try and forget about the whole thing. I took out an awesome tasting pizza from the pizza oven and served it to the hungry customer that had ordered it. The customer himself was a handsome, tall man, and he looked like he had just jumped out of a comic book or something. He was the kind of the guy that really stood out from the crowd, and you'd always notice him wherever he'd go.

Little did I know that the good looking customer whom had ordered the pizza...

Was actually the top player of the Murder Mystery 2 server!

What luck!

If luck was food, then I'd probably be really, really obese right about now!

"Here you go, sir. One pepperoni madness with cheese stuffing on the crust." I said softly.

"Hey... aren't you Noob?" the customer said.

"Yeah... how'd you know me?"

"I saw you on the Murder Mystery 2 server before... I'm actually the top player from that server."

"Whoah! Dude... your timing couldn't have been better! You're exactly the person I needed right now to solve a case that had went cold on this server!" I said happily.

"Yeah... I know all about that. The mysterious string of murders at the restaurant, right?" he asked me.

I leaned back in surprise at the customer's answer. I knew he was a great detective and all that, but I didn't know he was that good! I was pretty sure that Santy and I were the only people on the server who knew about that case! Well, us and the police, of course.

"Y-you... know about that..?"

"Of course! I wouldn't be the top player at the Murder Mystery 2 server if I didn't, now would I? The name's Bruce, by the way. Bruce Wade."

"Bruce Wade? Funny name..." I said softly.

Bruce let out a friendly chuckle and smiled.

"Yeah, people tend to say that a lot about my name. Anyway, you still wanna solve that case?" he asked.

"Of course! You see, the thing is, the only person who would ever believe me was my old manager, Santy! But he's gone missing now, and no one's gonna believe my story, but luckily you're here so--"

"Whoah, whoah, whoah, dude... settle down. Let's try to talk about this calmly, okay?" Bruce said slowly.

I took a deep breath and nodded my head. Bruce offered me to sit across him from the table and that's when I told him the whole story.

From the first time we suddenly saw the five former robbers get jobs at the pizza place...

To the time when Rojack told me about his story...

To when the mysterious murders first started...

To when I questioned Lombard about his history with the Christmas Grouch...

All the way to the present events.

Bruce simply listened closely as I told him everything's that happened so far.

He didn't say a single word as I was telling him the story. He just kept nodding and took some notes using his phone. After I had told him everything that had happened, he took in a deep breath and nodded his head silently again.

"Phew! That's a lot to take in now, isn't it?" he finally said.

"Yeah! And that's all of it! That's what

happened. So what do you think, Bruce? Where do you think Santy is now? And Rojack?" I asked him.

Bruce shook his head and smiled.

"Noob, you're looking at this whole case the wrong way. You're looking for Rojack because you think he's the Christmas Grouch, right?" Bruce said.

"Yeah! I mean, he is the Christmas Grouch, isn't he?"

"Of course he is. But you also told me that the Christmas Grouch has the ability to change skins because of how many Robux he has, right?" Bruce said.

"Uh... yeah."

"Don't you think it's a bit of a coincidence that Lombard, the former robber you just talked to last night was killed, and now Rojack and Santy have gone missing too?"

"Yes! I know that the Christmas Grouch is behind that murder, I'm sure of it! We just gotta look for Rojack!"

"That's the thing, Noob. We don't go around looking for Rojack... because he's already changed skins! He's probably killed Santy too, which explains why Santy suddenly 'quit' his job! He never quit! And the new manager right now... is the real Christmas Grouch!"

My eyes widened after hearing Bruce's explanation. He was right! It was under my nose all along! The Christmas Grouch probably changed his skin again, this time to a new manager! Which explains why Rojack had gone missing... and why Santy's missing too!

"Whoah... you're right! You're really smart, Bruce." I said.

Bruce flashed a smile my way and stood up from his chair.

"Hey, I wouldn't be the top player on the Roblox Murder Mystery 2 server if I didn't have the brains for it now, would I? Let's go ask this new 'manager' a few questions, shall we, Noob?"

I quickly stood up from my seat and nodded my head at Bruce.

"With pleasure."

Entry # 12:

Caught Red Handed!

Bruce Wade, the top player from the Murder Myster 2 server and I kicked the door down that lead to the manager's office inside the pizza restaurant. Inside, the new manager sat calmly on his leather chair, and he seemed genuinely surprised at his two new visitors after we kicked the door down.

"H-hey... w-what the..?! What is the meaning of this?!" he shouted out.

"The jig is up, 'new manager'! You're not the new manager of this pizza restaurant... We know who you are! Just admit it!" Bruce said as he pointed his finger towards the manager.

"Yeah, just admit it already! You're the Christmas Grouch, aren't you?" I said.

The man's eyes widened after hearing both of our accusations against him.

"The Christmas Grouch?! What are you talking about?"

"You're the same person who killed all of the pizza restaurant's employees a few days ago! Admit it!" Bruce said angrily.

The manager laughed and crossed his arms.

"Such bold claims! Do you have any proof?"

Bruce and I suddenly looked at each other and shook our heads.

"Well... no... we don't have any proof... but we know you're guilty!" I said aloud.

The manager let out an evil sounding laugh

before he smiled, showing his dark, yellow teeth.

"Then you can't catch me for anything. You have no proof! Now get out of my office right now before I call the police!" he said angrily.

"Wait! I have proof that you truly are the Christmas Grouch!" Bruce said.

"Where? Go on, I want to see it!" the manager said.

"Why is there a cigar on the pocket of your suit, Mr. Manager?" Bruce said as he pointed to a small cigar on the manager's pocket.

"Y-yeah... so..? That doesn't prove anything!"

"But it does! No one in the Work at a Pizza Place server has ever smoked before! And Noob told me about Rojack and Lombard... and how they said that you always had a cigar when they saw you at the Jailbreak server! There's only one guy who carries a cigar around with him all the time... and that man is none other than the Christmas Grouch!" Bruce said victoriously.

The manager shook his head and sneered at both of us.

"Fine! You got me! I am the Christmas Grouch and I killed all those guys! But who cares? There aren't any cops around anyway! They're not about to believe you just because you saw a cigar on my pocket!" he said.

"Oh... I think they'll believe us, alright." Bruce said before he reached out for his phone inside his pocket. He clicked on a button that was on the side of his phone, and it repeated the entire conversation that we just had with the Christmas Grouch, including his open confession.

"W-what..?! You were recording this whole conversation the entire time?!" the Christmas Grouch said nervously.

"Of course! A good detective always records key conversations." Bruce said before he winked and smiled at the Christmas Grouch.

"Curse youuuu!" the Christmas Grouch cried out.

"Tell me this, Christmas Grouch... Why? Why did you do it? Why did you kill all those people and why do you hate Christmas so much anyway?" I asked him.

The Christmas Grouch shook his head and sneered at me once again.

"Oh please! Shut up with all of that goody-two shoes Christmas stuff! Christmas is terrible, kid! I hate it! Everyone pretends to be nice and gives presents, but none of them really care about each other for the rest of the year! Christmas was also the time that my parents went away for a vacation and never came back! I hate Christmas! It's terrible!" the Christmas Grouch said.

I let out a deep sigh after hearing the Christmas Grouch's story. I guess I kind of couldn't blame him for acting that way. He had a lot of bad memories on Christmas... but still! That was still no excuse for all of his terrible actions!

"Look, dude... I kind of get what you're saying. I can see why you dislike Christmas so much... that's not an excuse for killing people and trying to ruin Christmas for an entire server! Instead of focusing on the bad things that happened to you on Christmas, you should be enjoying the good things that Christmas brings to everyone! Christmas is an awesome time, filled with cheer and joy! Don't focus on the past, but put yourself in the present instead! Don't be such a grouch!" I said.

"Well... it's too late for that! You guys already got me. It doesn't matter anymore!" the

Christmas Grouch said.

"We'll just turn you in to the cops and we'll see what the court will do about you, my friend." Bruce said calmly.

Entry # 13:

Merry Pizza-- I mean, Christmas! Merry Christmas!

Bruce Wade and I quickly turned in the Christmas Grouch to the local police of the Work at a Pizza Place server. As it turned out, the people he actually killed were just banned from playing the game, but the bans were instantly lifted once the Christmas Grouch admitted committing all of his crimes.

Hey, this is a game, what did you think happened anyway? That they really died or something?

Of course not!

Eventually, everyone got back together at the pizza restaurant...

Santy, Jonesy, Bruce Wade, Rojack, Cobra, Conard, Lombard, Jackson... and some few other minor characters which I totally forgot about. Sorry about that guys!

Everybody gathered around the pizza restaurant on Christmas eve, and Santy treated all of the customers out, including the employees too, to some free pizzas! Imagine that! Free pizzas for everybody!

It was totally awesome!

Everyone had a great time!

There were Christmas lights glistening in the windows, children singing some Christmas songs just outside the restaurant, and even a big old Christmas tree with a large star shining brightly on top. Everyone was having a great time, and everything turned out just fine in the end.

Apparently, the Christmas Grouch was probably the only person who was having another really, really bad Christmas, though.

The police decided to ban him from ever playing Roblox again, and threw him behind bars for a total of five years for all of his crazy crimes against the server!

In some kind of crazy attempt to escape his sentence, he even said that he wasn't the Christmas Grouch and that his real name was "Kaerfiren".

Strangely enough, that name seemed really familiar to me for some reason...

I could have sworn that I heard or seen that name before!

But whatever, it's not important anymore. Kaerfiren, or The Christmas Grouch, or whatever it is he wants to call himself, was behind bars, and could never play any Roblox game again!

But who knows... he might just find a way to escape! You can never tell with a sneaky and crafty guy like that!

But until that time, he's going to have to wait inside his cold prison cell and think about all the terrible things he's done.

And as for us?

We're enjoying Christmas, and I think this is just the beginning!

"Bleh! This pizza is terrible!" Bruce said as he took a bite off of his super spicy japaleno pizza.

Everyone inside the restaurant laughed as he gulped down glass after glass full of water.

Jonesy had played a prank on Bruce and told him that the spicy japaleno pizza was the pizza that he had ordered before. Apparently, Bruce found out the hard way that you couldn't really trust Jonesy.

"Jonesy, you j-jerk!" Bruce said as his face lit up like a Christmas tree.

"Merry Christmas, Bruce!" Jonesy said as he handed him a glass of milk.

"Hey, is everyone having a great time?" Santy said as he suddenly walked into the restaurant carrying several more boxes of hot and steamy pizza.

Everyone nodded their heads and gave the portly man a thumbs up.

"Dude, Santy... you should seriously dress up as Santa Claus! I mean, you totally look like him! You know, with the big belly and the white beard and all!" I said as I took a bite of some of my cheesy deluxe pizza.

"Nah... I think I'll do that next year though!

For now, let's just enjoy all of the festivities!" Santy said.

I couldn't agree more.

And that's pretty much how the story ends!

That's how I went from a normal pizza restaurant employee...

To a totally awesome detective that solved the case of the Christmas Grouch!

Well, to be fair, I didn't solve the case by myself... I had a little help from Bruce Wade, the number one player from the Murder Mystery 2 server.

But still! What mattered in the end is that Christmas was saved for the entire server and that the Christmas Grouch was behind bars for good!

Merry Christmas everyone!

The End.

If you enjoyed this book, please leave a review on Amazon! It would really help me with the series.

Best,

Robloxia Kid